GOLF

THROUGH THE EYES
OF A CHILD

Written by
Dominique DeSerres

Illustrated by
Aga Kubish

Published by
Golf Distillery - Extracting the Essence of Golf

ISBN: 978-1-7774183-1-1 (eBook)
ISBN: 978-1-7774183-0-4 (Paperback)
ISBN: 978-1-7774183-2-8 (Hardcover)

Illustrated by Aga Kubish

Written by Dominique DeSerres
Saint-Bruno-de-Montarville, Quebec, Canada

Golf Distillery

Hi, my name is Henry!

Join me as I walk you through the great game of golf
and explain what it means to me.

First of all, I like golf because
it takes place in a giant park.

You can play in the wind or in the rain
—but under a clear blue sky is best.

Don't get me wrong, I enjoy my screen time
and playing with my toys at home...

but summer days are meant to be spent outside.

I can form a group with up to three of my friends
when I play golf. It is called a foursome.

We all remain silent whenever someone is hitting
because it requires a lot of concentration.
After a good hit, we can say, "nice shot!"

Sure, golf can be serious at times,
but while we walk to our balls we can share
and laugh at the latest story or joke.

"So these golfers find a genie lamp
and are granted 3 wishes..."

My grandparents like to play golf too.
That means I can play with them AND my mom or dad
all at the same time!

We can play a competitive match or just for fun.
Doing activities with my family
is very precious to me.

My grandfather is a very good golfer.
He teaches me the best tips he has learned over the years.

He also reminds me that every single shot counts,
even the short putts.

The game of golf has variety since
no two consecutive shots are identical.

Golf courses themselves are also unique as
each course is different from the next.

See, I rarely hit the exact same shot twice in a row.

That means playing golf is always challenging
and never boring.

For example, with my driver,

I try to hit the ball as far forward as I can,

like it's a cannonball

shooting off into the distance.

Then, with my irons and wedges,

I aim for the ball to land very close to the flag.

It can feel like I'm shooting an arrow

straight into the bullseye.

Finally, with my putter,

I try to make the ball disappear into the hole.

When the ball hits the bottom of the cup,
it makes the sweetest sound,

especially when it travelled
a great distance before getting there.

As you can see, you get to make
a lot of decisions when you play golf.

Every time you walk up to your ball,
you need to choose the club you want to use
and the type of shot you want to hit.

You need to be smart about those decisions, too.

Sometimes it pays to be aggressive and to go for it,
but sometimes it's better to play it safe!

That's because the goal in golf
is to complete every hole using the fewest strokes.
The lower the number the better.

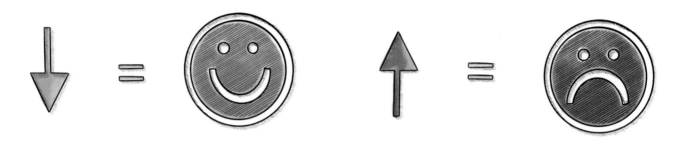

Hole	1	2	3	4	5	6	7	8	9	OUT	10	11	12	13	14	15	16	17	18	IN	TOTAL	

All in all, a round of golf gives you 18 holes to play
and should last under 4 hours.

Indeed, 18 holes to play well, or try to improve.

Hole		1	2	3	4	5	6	7	8	9	OUT

10	11	12	13	14	15	16	17	18	IN	TOTAL		

Even when you play badly in the first few holes,
you can't give up. Every hole is a new start
and a different journey from the last.

You can even ride a little cart on a golf course.

I like to hold the wheel in my hands and pretend
that I'm driving all by myself, which is so much fun.

My dad prefers to walk and carry his clubs
on his shoulders when he plays,

but I enjoy taking little breaks in the shade
from time to time.

There are many rules in golf,
even if there are no referees watching you play.

That's right.
Nobody blows a whistle
or gives you a red card if a rule is broken.

However, that doesn't mean cheating is allowed.
Instead, golfers call penalties on themselves.

By keeping the game fair for everyone,
golf teaches you to behave honourably toward others
and to be true to yourself.

The golfing community has been enjoying
the same sport for hundreds of years
and you can find us all over the world.

It was even played
on the surface of the Moon.

Plus, I am sure people will be playing golf
for hundreds of years into the future.

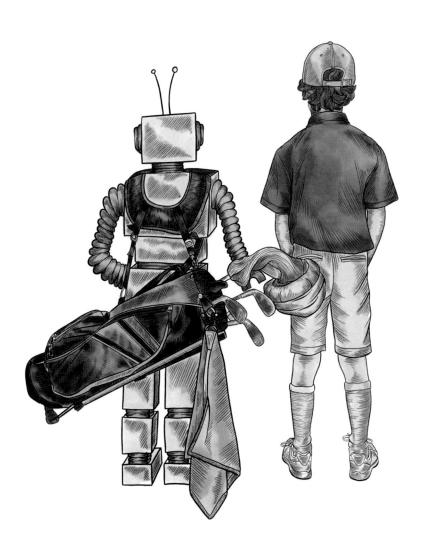

It may even be played by robots
or on Mars someday.

Oh, and before I finish, did I mention how calm
and peaceful golf can be?

When I play early in the morning,
my shoes sometimes leave footprints on the wet grass.

When I play at dusk, I can witness the sunset
and all of the beautiful colours that light up the sky.

I can feel the cooler air creeping in and can hear the birds
and insects chirping as they get ready for bed.

Finally, a round of golf ends
with the last putt on the last green.

We then remove our hats, thank our playing partners for
their company, shake hands (or give an embrace),
and walk off the course.

After all of this exercise, I like to sit down
and enjoy a refreshing beverage.

My dad will usually order a cold beer,
but I prefer a root beer.

There you have it.
That's why I like to play golf.

Have fun out there
and remember to leave the course
in the same condition it was when you found it.

Made in the USA
Las Vegas, NV
08 March 2024

86908132R00021